Brainy
BRITTANYS

GENTLE! OBEDIENT! KEEN!   STRONG! ALERT! UNTIRING!

ABDO
Publishing Company

Katherine Hengel

Consulting Editor, Diane Craig, M.A./Reading Specialist

Published by ABDO Publishing Company
8000 West 78th Street, Edina, Minnesota 55439.

Printed in the United States.

Editor: Pam Price
Content Developer: Nancy Tuminelly
Cover and Interior Design and Production:
   Anders Hanson, Mighty Media
Illustrations: Bob Doucet
Photo Credits: Shutterstock, iStock Photo, Peter Arnold Inc.
(p. 7, © Biosphoto / Sement Didier)

Library of Congress Cataloging-in-Publication Data

Hengel, Katherine.
  Brainy brittanys / Katherine Hengel ; illustrated by Bob
Doucet.
    p. cm. -- (Dog daze)
  ISBN 978-1-60453-616-4
  1. Brittany spaniel--Juvenile literature. I. Doucet, Bob, ill.
II. Title.

  SF429.B78H46 2009
  636.752'4--dc22
                           2008040269

Super SandCastle™ books are created by a team of
professional educators, reading specialists, and content
developers around five essential components—phonemic
awareness, phonics, vocabulary, text comprehension, and
fluency—to assist young readers as they develop reading
skills and strategies and increase their general
knowledge. All books are written, reviewed, and leveled
for guided reading, early reading intervention, and
Accelerated Reader® programs for use in shared, guided,
and independent reading and writing activities to support
a balanced approach to literacy instruction.

CONTENTS

The
BRITTANY

Brittanys are medium-sized bird dogs. They are athletic and strong but not heavy. Brittanys have smart faces and long legs. Brittanys come in many colors. Their coats are usually orange and white.

Brittanys are good family dogs. But they need a lot of exercise to be happy.

FACIAL FEATURES

Head

Brittanys have round skulls and straight **snouts**.

Teeth and Mouth

Brittanys have strong, sharp teeth to help them hunt. They have thin, tight-fitting lips.

Eyes

A Brittany's oval eyes are often amber or hazel, depending on its coat color.

Ears

Their triangle-shaped ears sit high on their heads. The fur on their ears is wavy.

4

BODY BASICS

Size

Brittanys can grow to be 21 inches (53 cm) tall. They weigh about 40 pounds (18 kg).

Build

A Brittany is typically quite athletic, compact, and solidly built without being heavy.

Tail

Brittanys can have short tails or long tails. Some owners have their dogs' tails shortened.

Legs and Feet

Brittanys have long legs, so they can run fast. Their feet are round, and they have tight toe pads.

COAT & COLOR

Brittany Fur

Brittanys have fine, light fur that stays close to their bodies. Their fur is slightly shorter and lighter near their heads than it is on their bodies. Most of the time, their coats are orange and white. They can also be black and white, **liver** and white, or **roan**.

LIVER FUR

WHITE COAT WITH LIVER MARKINGS

Brittanys come in many different colors and coats.
The photos on these pages show just a few examples.

BLACK FUR

WHITE FUR

ORANGE FUR

WHITE COAT WITH
BLACK MARKINGS

WHITE COAT WITH
ORANGE MARKINGS

ROAN COAT WITH
ORANGE MARKINGS

HEALTH & CARE

Life Span

Most Brittanys live to be 10 to 13 years old. Some live up to 15 years, however.

Grooming

Regular brushing will keep a Brittany's coat in good condition. Check and clean their ears carefully, especially when they have been running through bushes or long grass. This **breed** is a light shedder.

VET'S CHECKLIST

- Have your Brittany spayed or neutered.

- Visit a vet for regular checkups.

- Ask your vet which foods are right for your Brittany.

- Make sure your Brittany gets plenty of exercise in wide-open spaces.

- Brittanys should not be left alone outside unless they are inside a fenced-in yard.

- Clean your Brittany's teeth and ears once a week.

EXERCISE & TRAINING

Activity Level

Brittanys are very active and enthusiastic. They require frequent exercise and plenty of room to run. They make good house pets as long as they receive daily mental and physical exercise. They should **socialize** with other dogs on a regular basis.

Obedience

Brittanys are very **obedient** and easy to train. Sensitive and softhearted, these jolly dogs like to please their owners!

A Few Things You'll Need

A **leash** lets your Brittany know that you are the boss. With a leash, you can guide your dog where you want it to go. Most cities require that dogs be on leashes when they are outside.

A **collar** is a strap that goes around your Brittany's neck. You can attach a leash to the collar to take your dog on walks. You should also attach an **identification tag** with your home address. If your dog ever gets lost, people will know where it lives.

Toys keep your Brittany healthy and happy. Brittanys like to chase and chew on them.

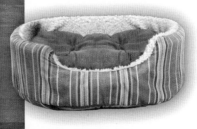

A **dog bed** will help your pet feel safe and comfortable at night.

ATTITUDE & INTELLIGENCE

Personality

Brittanys are easy to train, sensitive, and sweet natured. They are happiest when they are running, hunting, and playing. Brittanys are quick and curious.

Intellect

Brittanys are very smart, which makes them wonderful companions. Most Brittanys show a great ability to communicate with their owners.

All About Me

Hi! My name is Molly. I'm a Brittany. I just wanted to let you know a few things about me. I made some lists below of things I like and dislike. Check them out!

Things I Like

- Running outside in all kinds of weather
- Going on long hunting trips
- Playing with other Brittanys
- Learning new hunting or training techniques
- Giving big hugs and kisses to my owners
- Pointing to birds in a field

Things I Dislike

- Being harshly scolded
- Hanging out in small spaces
- Staying indoors all day
- Being ignored

LITTERS & PUPPIES

Litter Size

Female Brittanys usually give birth to six to ten puppies.

Diet

Newborn pups drink their mother's milk. They can begin to eat soft puppy food when they are about four weeks old.

Growth

Brittany puppies should stay with their mothers until they are eight weeks old. A Brittany will be almost full grown when it is a year old. It will continue to grow, however, until it is two years old.

BUYING A BRITTANY

Choosing a Breeder

It's best to buy a puppy from a **breeder**, not a pet store. When you visit a dog breeder, ask to see the mother and father of the puppies. Make sure the parents are healthy, friendly, and well behaved.

Picking a Puppy

Choose a puppy that isn't too **aggressive** or too shy. If you crouch down, some of the puppies may want to play with you. One of them might be the right one for you!

Is It the Right Dog for You?

Buying a dog is a big decision. You'll want to make sure your new pet suits your lifestyle.

Get out a piece of paper. Draw a line down the middle.

Read the statements listed here. Each time you agree with a statement from the left column, make a mark on the left side of your paper. When you agree with a statement from the right column, make a mark on the right side of your paper.

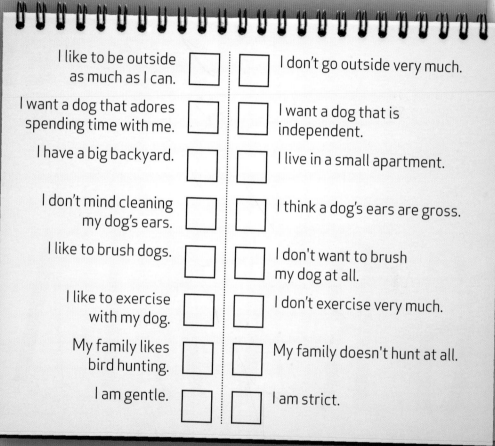

I like to be outside as much as I can.	☐ ☐	I don't go outside very much.
I want a dog that adores spending time with me.	☐ ☐	I want a dog that is independent.
I have a big backyard.	☐ ☐	I live in a small apartment.
I don't mind cleaning my dog's ears.	☐ ☐	I think a dog's ears are gross.
I like to brush dogs.	☐ ☐	I don't want to brush my dog at all.
I like to exercise with my dog.	☐ ☐	I don't exercise very much.
My family likes bird hunting.	☐ ☐	My family doesn't hunt at all.
I am gentle.	☐ ☐	I am strict.

If you made more marks on the left side than on the right side, a Brittany may be the right dog for you! If you made more marks on the right side of your paper, you might want to consider another breed.

THE SOFTHEARTED POINTER

Brittanys come from the Brittany province of France. We can see Brittanys in French paintings and **tapestries** from the 17th century! It is believed that Brittanys are related to English pointing dogs and spaniel **breeds** from Spain.

Today Brittanys are one of the most popular bird-hunting **breeds**. These loving, clever dogs were originally called Brittany spaniels. But the word *spaniel* was recently removed. Why? Because Brittanys don't chase their prey like spaniels do. Instead, they point.

THE BRITTANY AND THE BEAR

One day, Gary Paterna was walking on a trail through the woods with his nine-year-old Brittany, Tok. Gary and Tok had walked on that trail many, many times together. All of a sudden, Gary heard a loud roar.

It was a female grizzly bear! One of her cubs was with her
too. The **protective** mother bear charged down the path and
knocked Gary over. But instead of running away, Tok stayed by
Gary and distracted the bear. Eventually, the grizzly and her cub
retreated up the path, and Gary and Tok ran away to safety.

FIND THE BRITTANY

A

B

C

D

THE BRITTANY QUIZ

1. Brittanys are not athletic. **True or false?**

2. Brittanys have sharp teeth that they use when they are hunting. **True or false?**

3. Brittanys like to please their owners. **True or false?**

4. Brittanys do not need much exercise. **True or false?**

5. It's difficult to train a Brittany. **True or false?**

6. Brittanys point at their prey. **True or false?**

Answers: 1) false 2) true 3) true 4) false 5) false 6) true

GLOSSARY

aggressive – likely to attack or confront.

breed – a group of animals or plants with common ancestors. A *breeder* is someone whose job is to breed certain animals or plants.

liver – a grayish reddish brown.

obedient – willing to follow rules, orders, or directions.

protective – guarding someone or something from harm or danger.

retreat – to move back or withdraw from a difficult situation.

roan – a base color, such as red, black, or brown, lightened by white hairs.

snout – the projecting nose or jaws of an animal's head.

socialize – to be with others and enjoy their company.

tapestry – a woven cloth with pictures or patterns in it.